How To Catch a Fish

by John Frank

ILLUSTRATED BY Peter Sylvada

A NEAL PORTER BOOK
ROARING BROOK PRESS
NEW MILFORD, CONNECTICUT

For Roger
—J.F.

For my father and my uncle, who both taught me during
our many years of fishing the Baja together.
—P.S.

Text copyright © 2007 by John Frank
Illustrations copyright © 2007 by Peter Sylvada
A Neal Porter Book
Published by Roaring Brook Press
Roaring Brook Press is a division of Holtzbrinck Publishing Holdings Limited Partnership
143 West Street, New Milford, Connecticut 06776
www.roaringbrookpress.com

Distributed in Canada by H. B. Fenn and Company, Ltd.

Library of Congress Cataloging-in-Publication Data
Frank, John.
How to catch a fish / by John Frank ; illustrated by Peter Sylvada. — 1st ed.
p. cm.
"A Neal Porter book."
Summary: Rhyming text and illustrations describe the ways fish are caught in various locations around the world.
ISBN-13: 978-1-59643-163-8   ISBN-10: 1-59643-163-6
[1. Fishing—Fiction. 2. Stories in rhyme.] I. Sylvada, Peter, ill. II. Title.
PZ8.3.F84793Ho 2007   [E]—dc22   2006032184

Roaring Brook Press books are available for special promotions and premiums.
For details, contact: Director of Special Markets, Holtzbrinck Publishers.

Printed in China   First edition October 2007
Book design by Jennifer Browne
10 9 8 7 6 5 4 3 2 1

This is how to catch a fish . . .

Within the early hours of day
we launch our small boat from the beach
and spread our net out on the bay,
then shortly after drag it back
upon the shore, and sort the catch—
anchovy, tuna, kingfish, jack—
and if we're lucky there'll be lots
to fill the village supper pots.

Seine fishing, Turtle Bay, Tobago

Past jagged rocks and chunks of boulders—

banks of stone that tame the tide

along the mighty river's shoulders

just before it joins the sea—

we troll our bait for silver salmon

as they fight the current's motion,

swimming upstream from the ocean,

tugged by instinct, miles and miles,

to spawn where they themselves were born.

Angling for coho, Columbia River, Washington

With bits of feather, yarn, and thread,
we fashion insects, small and light,
that look so real it seems as if
they'll set their tiny wings awhirl
and in the morning haze take flight.
In rubber boots that reach our thighs
we wade out in the coursing stream,
and with quick wrist-flicks of our rods
we cast, in shimmering arcs, the flies,
which, once our lengths of line play out,
just scarcely graze the water's face—
enough to tease the hungry trout.

Fly-fishing, Gap of Dunloe, Ireland

We chop a hole in the Arctic ice,

and crouched in layers of skins and fur

to shun the frigid weather—*b-rrr-rr*—

we bait our hooks and lower our lines

and jig them, up and down, to stir

the fish below—but if they're near,

we'll sometimes use a well-aimed spear.

Ice fishing, Baffin Island, Nunavut

Around the neck of a cormorant

we've clamped a ring—a metal collar—

and to this we tie a leash.

In our flat-bottomed boat at night

we paddle up the river, where

our metal basket's flickering fire—

its bright hypnotic dancing light—

draws sweetfish near . . . and as they follow,

overboard the leashed bird dives

to seize its prey, which we then take—

big fish the ringed throat cannot swallow.

Ukai, *(cormorant fishing)*, *Nagara River, Japan*

Standing at the ocean beach
on wet sand hemmed by hissing foam,
we scan the surf to spot the breach
between the waves before they break—
the cleft of sea where game fish roam.
To there we'll cast our rigs from shore—
our hooks and baits above the weights
that quickly to the bottom sink,
our gold-spoon lures that flash and wink—
and catch some fish to carry home.

Surf casting, Montauk Point, New York

We hide—among the reeds that
by the riverbank so thickly grow—
or float on water, shallow, slow,
in logboats crafted long and narrow,
waiting with a watching eye
to take the fish with bow and arrow.

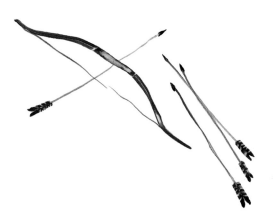

Watu (logboat) fishing, Okavango River, Namibia

In snorkeling mask and fins, and armed

to fire a spear or sharp harpoon,

we hunt along the reef below

the surface of the green lagoon,

for barracuda, dogtooth tuna—

challenged by our lungs to dive

as deep as one held breath will bear . . .

before we must come up for air.

Spearfishing, New Caledonia, southwest Pacific

We strip the bark from limbs of fir
and make them into poles as tall
as three men head to toe combined,
and lash to them a white-oak hoop—
a supple branch shaped over fire—
and netting from wild iris twined.
Our dip nets now complete, we climb
the rocks between the steep cliff walls,
and swing the long poles through the roar
of rapids carving canyon floor—
to catch the fish that scale the falls.

Dip-netting, Ishi Pishi Falls, California

Propelled by currents swift and strong,

our fishwheel rotates round and round,

its soft metallic hollow sound

as rhythmic as a beaten drum,

three giant baskets scooping up

the sockeye, steelhead, coho, chum

and dropping them inside a pen—

then circling back for more again.

Fishwheel, Fraser Canyon, British Columbia

Through rags of morning mist we set out

on a lake as smooth as glass;

a few stone-skips beyond the shore

we cast our spinnerbaits in grass

that grows among the shallows, and

we let them sink, then reel them in—

with slow and steady turns as patient

as a watch's second hand—

to lure the lurking largemouth bass.

Angling for bass, Chattahoochee National Forest, Georgia

We strap on sturdy harnesses

and brace ourselves in bolted chairs

to angle for a fish whose size

can dwarf gigantic grizzly bears:

blue marlin. One once caught by hook

weighed nearly eighteen hundred pounds

(though some would say because it took

more than one man to reel it in,

it shouldn't grace the record book).

It's every deep-sea angler's wish,

a battle packaged as a fish,

a leaping, thrashing tug-of-war,

that strains to snap your rod in two,

to drag your line until it melts,

a fight for all you've got—and more.

And when we haul one from the sea

we sound our loud triumphant cheers,

and gauge its length and girth and weight—

then set the wondrous creature free.

Deep-sea fishing, Kona, Hawaii

As sunrise tints the eastern sky,

the two of us walk down the pier

with fishing poles, one short, one tall,

and tackle boxes, big and small.

Above the ocean, way up high,

we find our spot along the rails;

I hope I'll be the very first

to get a nibble, then a bite,

to reel in from the sea the right

to beam with pride as passersby

who peer in all the anglers' pails

admire the first fish of the day,

light glinting off its shiny scales. . . .

Pier fishing, Gulf coast, northwest Florida

We slack our reels to free some line,

and as I mull which rig to tie,

a knowing wink escapes his eye;

I make my choice of hook and weight,

we fasten them, we set our bait,

then raise our rods, set loose our lines,

above the ocean, way up high,

the two of us, my dad and I. . . .

And that is how to catch a fish.